MR 0 8 '73

Hands
Are for Holding

THE SENSE OF TOUCH

Katherine Hengel

Consulting Editor, Diane Craig, M.A./Reading Specialist

A Division of ABDO

ABDO
Publishing Company

visit us at www.abdopublishing.com

Published by ABDO Publishing Company, a division of ABDO, P.O. Box 398166, Minneapolis, Minnesota 55439. Copyright © 2012 by Abdo Consulting Group, Inc. International copyrights reserved in all countries. No part of this book may be reproduced in any form without written permission from the publisher. SandCastle™ is a trademark and logo of ABDO Publishing Company.

Printed in the United States of America, North Mankato, Minnesota
102011
012012

 PRINTED ON RECYCLED PAPER

Editor: Liz Salzmann
Content Developer: Nancy Tuminelly
Cover and Interior Design and Production: Oona Gaarder-Juntti, Mighty Media, Inc.
Photo Credits: BananaStock, Digital Vision, Hoby Fin, Shutterstock, Thinkstock

Library of Congress Cataloging-in-Publication Data
Hengel, Katherine.
  Hands are for holding : the sense of touch / Katherine Hengel.
     p. cm. -- (All about your senses)
  ISBN 978-1-61783-198-0
  1. Hand--Juvenile literature. 2. Senses and sensation--Juvenile literature. I. Title.
  QM548.H46 2012
  612.8--dc23
                          2011023493

SandCastle™ Level: Transitional

SandCastle™ books are created by a team of professional educators, reading specialists, and content developers around five essential components—phonemic awareness, phonics, vocabulary, text comprehension, and fluency—to assist young readers as they develop reading skills and strategies and increase their general knowledge. All books are written, reviewed, and leveled for guided reading, early reading intervention, and Accelerated Reader® programs for use in shared, guided, and independent reading and writing activities to support a balanced approach to literacy instruction. The SandCastle™ series has four levels that correspond to early literacy development. The levels are provided to help teachers and parents select appropriate books for young readers.

Emerging Readers
(no flags)

Beginning Readers
(1 flag)

Transitional Readers
(2 flags)

Fluent Readers
(3 flags)

Table of Contents

Hands

Are for Holding

Hands are special. They can do a lot! It's fun to hold hands with friends. Julia and Kate hold hands and lean back. They trust each other!

What else are hands for?
What can hands sense or feel?

Hands

Are for Feeling

Abby is holding her neighbor's pet bunny. The bunny feels soft and warm.

We use our hands to feel the things around us. Our skin is covered with **sense receptors**. They send messages to our brains. That's how we feel things!

Our Sense of
Touch

Touch is one of our five senses. Our sense of touch exists wherever we have skin.

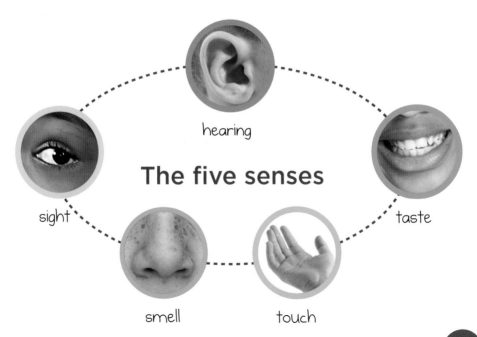

hearing

The five senses

sight

taste

smell

touch

Hands

Are for Playing

Robbie covered himself with sand! It's his favorite thing to do at the beach. He can feel the sand with his feet, body, and hands!

Our hands can feel **texture**. Sand feels **rough**.

11

Hands

Are for Washing

Hands can feel how hot or cold something is. Will washes his hands. The water is cold at first. But he can feel it starting to get warmer!

Hands can feel a lot!
What else can hands do?

Hands

Are for Reading

Karl is reading **braille**. He feels the words with his fingers! He reads at least one book every week.

Our fingers are very **sensitive**. There are about 100 **sense receptors** in each fingertip! People who are blind use their fingertips to read.

15

Hands

Are for Waving

Molly puts her hand out the car window. She waves good-bye to her teacher. You can also wave hello to someone.

Hands
Are for High Fives

Drew and Rick are on the same kickball team. Drew just scored! Drew runs over to Rick. They jump in the air for a high five!

Hands

Can Feel and Do a Lot!

Martin uses his hands to put on his wool hat. What do you think the hat feels like?

Facts About Touch

◆ Each **sense receptor** does one job. Most receptors **sense** heat, cold, pain, or **pressure**.

◆ It's important to feel pain! Pain tells you that something is wrong. It tells you to get help.

◆ The least **sensitive** part of the body is the middle of the back.

Touch Quiz

1. **Sense receptors** are not all over our skin. True or false?

2. Touch is one of our five senses. True or false?

3. Hands cannot feel how hot and cold things are. True or false?

4. Some people read with their hands. True or false?

Answers 1. False 2. True 3. False 4. True

Glossary

braille – a way of writing using raised dots that can be felt.

pressure – the force of something pressing against something else.

rough – not smooth or soft.

sense receptor – one of the tiny parts of the body that senses things, such as heat, and sends the information to the brain.

sensitive – able to feel and respond to slight changes.

texture – how rough or smooth something looks or feels.